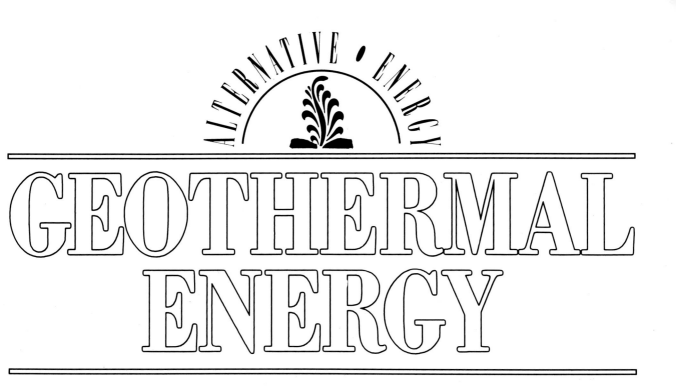

GEOTHERMAL ENERGY

GRAHAM RICKARD

Gareth Stevens Children's Books
MILWAUKEE

Titles in the Alternative Energy series:

Bioenergy
Geothermal Energy
Solar Energy
Water Energy
Wind Energy

For a free color catalog describing Gareth Stevens' list of high-quality children's books, call 1-800-341-3569 (USA) or 1-800-461-9120 (Canada).

Library of Congress Cataloging-in-Publication Data

Rickard, Graham.
    Geothermal energy / Graham Rickard.
        p. cm. — (Alternative energy)
    "First published in the United Kingdom, copyright 1990, by Wayland
(Publishers) Limited"—T.p. verso.
    Includes index.
    Summary: Explains how geothermal energy, natural heat from inside
the earth, can be used as a source of heat or to provide electricity.
    ISBN 0-8368-0708-1
    1. Geothermal engineering—Juvenile literature. [1. Geothermal
resources. 2. Geothermal engineering.] I. Title. II. Series:
Alternative energy (Milwaukee, Wis.)
TJ280.7.R53   1991
621.44—dc20   91-9262

North American edition first published in 1991 by

Gareth Stevens Children's Books
1555 North RiverCenter Drive, Suite 201
Milwaukee, Wisconsin 53212, USA

U.S. edition copyright © 1991 by Gareth Stevens, Inc. First published in the United Kingdom, copyright © 1990,
by Wayland (Publishers) Limited.

Picture Acknowledgements

Artwork by Nick Hawken

The publishers would like to thank the following for providing illustrations for this book: Energy Technology Support
Unit, 24, 25; Eye Ubiquitous, 21; Geoscience Features, 8, 13, 16, 19, 26; Hutchison, 11, 14; Photri, 27 (upper); Science
Photo Library, 18; Survival Anglia, 12, 17; Topham, cover, 20, 27 (lower); Zefa, 4, 5, 15.

Editors (UK): Paul Mason and William Wharfe
Editors (U.S.): Eileen Foran and John D. Rateliff
Designers: Charles Harford and David Armitage
Consultants: Mike Flood, Ph.D. and Jonathan Scurlock, Ph.D.

Printed in Italy

1 2 3 4 5 6 7 8 9 95 94 93 92 91

Contents

Words that appear in the glossary are printed in **boldface** type the first time they appear in the text.

WHY ALTERNATIVE ENERGY?

Energy is the ability to do work. All animals and plants need energy in order to live. All machines need energy to make them work. As the world's population increases and people use more machines, more energy is needed to power them. The world's demand for energy has increased by more than ten times since the beginning of the twentieth century.

Most of this energy is produced by burning one of three **fossil fuels** — oil, natural gas, and coal. But there is only so much fossil fuel in the world. Supplies that took millions of years to build up are being burned at the rate of over

On the crowded highways of Los Angeles, thousands of cars use up fuel and pollute the air with exhaust gases.

half a million tons an hour. At this rate, all the world's oil and gas will be gone by the year 2040.

Even worse, fossil fuels cause serious damage to the environment. When they burn, fossil fuels produce poisonous gases which turn into **acid rain**. Acid rain pollutes vast areas of the world, killing trees, fish, and wildlife. Some of these gases also contribute to the **greenhouse effect**, which is gradually warming up the Earth's **atmosphere**.

Because of all these problems, people all over the world are looking for alternative sources of energy. Some people see the use of **nuclear energy** as the best alternative to fossil fuels. But nuclear energy depends on supplies of uranium, which is even rarer than the fossil fuels we use now. Also, the pollution caused by nuclear energy is far more dangerous than anything produced by fossil fuels. So scientists and environmentalists are working together to come up with safe, clean, and renewable sources of energy.

There are many natural sources of energy all around us. The power of the Sun, wind, and moving

Oil rigs like this will disappear as an energy-hungry world uses up all its oil supplies.

water of tides and rivers all provide clean, renewable energy, if we can only come up with ways to use them. Another natural source of energy is **geothermal energy** that escapes from inside the Earth. This is a vast source of energy that we have only just begun to tap. Geothermal energy is already being used in several countries, and in the future it could play an important part in replacing fossil fuels.

THE HEAT BENEATH OUR FEET

Geothermal energy is the natural heat beneath the Earth's surface. The word *geothermal* comes from two ancient Greek words: *geo*, which means "of the Earth," and *therme*, which means "heat." Some of this heat has been trapped inside our planet since it was first formed. Scientists think that the Earth and the solar system were made out of a vast cloud of dust and gas floating in space. As particles in the cloud collided, they joined together and made the Sun and the planets. These collisions produced a lot of heat. The Earth was very hot when it first formed, over five billion years ago. The outside slowly cooled, but the inside stayed hot. It's still hot today because the weight of all that rock on top squeezes the core, making it red-hot.

A Cross Section of the Earth

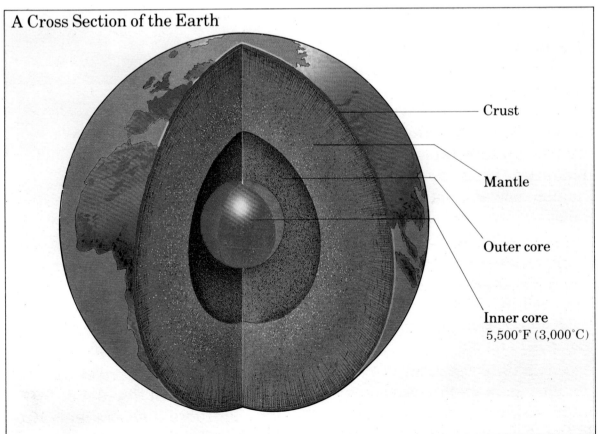

Crust

Mantle

Outer core

Inner core
5,500°F (3,000°C)

The Earth is hottest at its inner core, which scientists think is made of solid iron and iron alloys. The outer core is almost as hot and is made up of **molten** metals. Next comes the mantle, which is solid rock but still so hot that it is soft. Last of all comes the thin outer layer, like the skin of an onion, called the crust, the part we live on. Heat from the core escapes outward toward the cool crust. This is the heat that we call geothermal energy.

In some places the crust is very thin, and hot molten rock breaks through the surface to form volcanoes there. Volcanoes are one form of geothermal energy. The molten rock, or magma, in volcanoes can be as hot as 2,300°F (1,260°C). But volcanoes are too unpredictable and too dangerous for us to try to control and use as a source of energy.

Apart from volcanoes, there are many other places in the world where the Earth's heat reaches the surface. In some places in the Canary Islands, for example, you can easily burn your fingers just by scraping away some of the soil. Sometimes water is trapped underground among hot rocks. When it heats up and boils, it

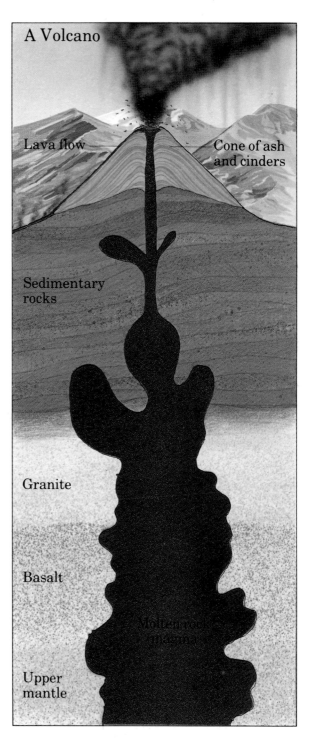

A Volcano

Lava flow

Cone of ash and cinders

Sedimentary rocks

Granite

Basalt

Molten rock magma

Upper mantle

Volcanoes are formed when molten rock is forced to the surface.

expands. The pressure of the expanding steam forces it to the surface, where it shoots high into the air to form a **geyser**.

THE HEAT BENEATH OUR FEET

The geysers in Yellowstone National Park are a popular tourist attraction.

Some geysers are really spectacular, and people come from far away to see them. One of the most famous is Old Faithful in Yellowstone National Park. This geyser erupts every 30 to 90 minutes, shooting hot water between 125 and 175 feet (38 to 53 m) into the air, amazing the crowds that gather to watch. In other places, where the underground pressure is not as great, like Hot Springs, Arkansas, geothermal energy produces hot springs and bubbling ponds of hot mud.

The Earth's heat is a source of natural energy that we could use to help replace fossil fuels. The amount of heat energy which reaches the Earth's surface is four times as much as the world needs. The main problem with geothermal energy is that it is spread over the entire world. The amount in any one area is usually too small to use. So geothermal energy can usually be used only in places where a lot of heat is close to the surface, such as the area around the Pacific known as the **Ring of Fire**.

About 80 countries throughout the world might be able to use geothermal energy. In places like Iceland and New Zealand, large underground stores of hot water occur naturally.

Underground supplies of hot water can be brought to the surface to heat houses, greenhouses, and swimming pools.

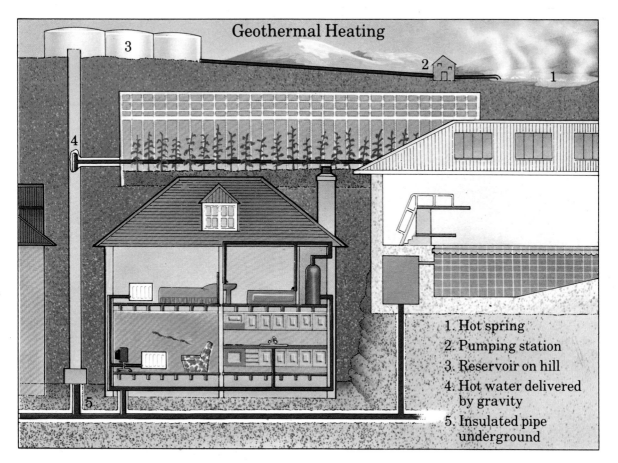

Geothermal Heating

1. Hot spring
2. Pumping station
3. Reservoir on hill
4. Hot water delivered by gravity
5. Insulated pipe underground

How Steam is Produced

1. The atoms have not yet been given much energy by the fire's heat, so they are not moving.

2. As the fire releases energy, the atoms begin to move and some of them escape as steam.

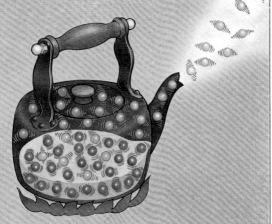

3. Once the water is boiling, more and more atoms bounce out of the water as steam.

Steam is made as the atoms in the water begin to bounce into the air.

This underground water can easily be pumped to the surface and used for heating homes, schools, and offices. Where there are no natural underground reservoirs, water can be pumped down deep holes into hot rocks and then brought back to the surface to be used for heating. Very hot water and steam can also be used to produce electricity.

Geothermal energy will never be able to provide all the energy the world needs. We can't power cars and airplanes with it. But we can use it to heat our homes and provide cities with electricity. Because geothermal energy is cheap, easy to use, and pollution-free, it could play an important part in our future.

The main reason that we have an energy crisis today is that we get almost all our energy from very few sources. In the future, we may **diversify** to use more and different kinds of energy — windmills to pump water, water wheels to power machinery, solar energy to make electricity, and hot springs to heat houses. Using a variety of energy sources makes us less dependent on any one of them and would also help cut down on pollution.

A geothermal power station at Svartsengi in Iceland. Local people swim in the warm lake, even when the air is very cold. In addition to being warm in the coldest weather, the water contains natural chemicals that help cure skin problems.

GEOTHERMAL ENERGY IN THE PAST

The idea of using the Earth's heat is not a new one. The very first users of geothermal energy were animals who used natural hot spots to help them survive the cold of winter. For example, Japanese monkeys spend their winters near hot springs. When it snows, the monkeys use the springs to keep warm. There are even hot springs on the ocean floor that support little colonies of life miles beneath the surface.

The people of ancient civilizations — the Greeks, the Japanese, and especially the Romans — also knew about, and used, hot

These Japanese monkeys survive the cold winter months by sitting in geothermal pools to keep warm.

The English town of Bath gets its name from the great bathhouses the Romans built there. The bathhouse ruins are still warmed by the same springs.

springs. The Romans built large public baths throughout their empire wherever there were natural hot springs. In many places, we can still see the ruins of their bathhouses today.

In Ibusuki, Japan, people like to relax in a bath of hot sand. The sand is heated by geothermal energy.

Natural hot water often contains high levels of **minerals**, such as sulfur, which were thought to be good for people. Some Roman baths became health resorts, or **spas**. A few of them are just as popular today as they were 2,000 years ago.

People put geothermal energy to work in other ways as well. For centuries, the Maori people of New Zealand have used rocks and water heated by geothermal

energy to cook their food. In Iceland, the people used the water from hot springs for cooking and for washing clothes. One famous medieval Icelander, the poet Snorri Sturluson, cut a channel so that water from a hot spring would flow under the floor of his house, keeping it warm during Iceland's bitter winters.

More recently, in 1894, the city of Boise, Idaho, became the first town to use geothermal wells for heating homes and factories. In Japan, hot water was used to heat greenhouses where food could be grown in winter. In the 1930s, Iceland began to use its supplies of naturally hot water to provide heat for people's homes on a large scale.

One problem with using geothermal energy is that hot water quickly cools off and loses its energy when taken away from its springs. This means that geothermal energy has to be used near the place where it is found. When the electric **generator** was invented in the nineteenth century, people began to use the energy in steam to produce electricity. Electricity can be used far away from where it is made. In 1904, an experiment at Larderello, Italy, showed that steam could produce enough electricity to light five light bulbs at once.

After this successful experiment, the Italians built a small power station. By the 1940s, it produced enough electricity to power an electric railway system. Today, New Zealand, Japan, the United States, and the Soviet Union all follow Italy's example.

The ancient Italian town of Larderello, home of the first electricity-producing geothermal power station.

ENERGY FROM HOT WATER

Most of the world's geothermal energy comes from large underground **reservoirs** of hot water. These natural reservoirs are called **aquifers**. They have formed over millions of years, as rainwater has seeped down through cracks and **porous** rocks, such as limestone. Porous rocks hold water inside in the same way that a sponge does. These rocks store water deep under the ground, on top of a layer of much hotter and harder nonporous rocks. The deeper the rocks, the hotter they are. They heat the water above them.

Water from below the surface rises to form hot springs.

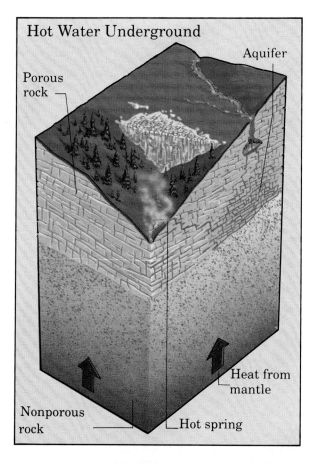

Hot Water Underground

Porous rock

Aquifer

Heat from mantle

Nonporous rock

Hot spring

Geysers often contain minerals, which form strange and colorful shapes when they reach the surface.

Most aquifers are about 8,200 feet (2,500 m) deep. Except in volcanic regions, the water temperature is rarely higher than the boiling point. This water is ideal for heating, and can mean a great saving in fuel costs. One problem is that heating systems for sharing the water among houses and shops are expensive to build and to run.

Sometimes the water rises to the surface on its own as geysers or hot springs. Usually, though, wells have to be dug so that the hot water can be pumped up from the aquifer. Once the water reaches the surface, powerful pumps are needed to circulate the water through a system of insulated pipes to the homes and shops that use the heat.

17

Sometimes minerals in the water, like sulfur, build up inside the pipes, blocking them. But despite such problems, the use of hot-water energy is catching on.

Today, homes in countries as far apart as France, Hungary, Japan, and New Zealand are warmed by geothermal energy. In Iceland, a volcanic island with large supplies of natural hot water, geothermal wells provide 80 percent of all heating. The country's capital, Reykjavik, has a system of hot-water pipes that runs under the streets and through people's houses. The hot

Despite its cold climate, this town in Iceland is famous for the tropical fruit it grows using heat from the Earth.

This greenhouse is heated by hot water, which is pumped from under the ground through pipes and radiators.

water is also used in the city's swimming pools, washing machines, and showers.

Iceland is near the North Pole, so the weather there is very cold. Even so, tropical fruits such as bananas and pineapples can be grown in greenhouses heated by natural hot water. Iceland has no fossil fuels of its own, so it is completely dependent on foreign imports for its gasoline, heating oil, and other petroleum products. Imported oil is very expensive, while geothermal energy costs only half as much as any other form of heating there.

To produce electricity, most power stations burn fuel to heat water, which turns into steam. The steam drives a **turbine**, which turns a generator to produce an electric current. Where natural steam from geothermal vents can be used, it saves an enormous amount of expensive fuel. Unfortunately, the steam must be very hot, at least 390°F (200°C), to produce electricity. There are very few aquifers where the ground water is hot enough.

However, several countries — including Italy, New Zealand, Japan, and the U.S. — are now generating electricity using the Earth's heat. The world's largest geothermal power stations are in the Little Geysers area of California. They produce enough electricity for 1.3 million people. In the Philippines, geothermal energy produces a third of all the nation's power needs, and many other countries are now building geothermal power stations.

These colorful pipes are part of an experimental geothermal power station in Hawaii, part of the Ring of Fire.

These chalk terraces at Pamukkale in Turkey are made of minerals from the water of the area's hot springs.

Although it uses no fuel, geothermal energy does have its own environmental problems. Underground supplies of hot water often contain dangerous minerals, such as ammonia, mercury, arsenic, and sulfur. If they are poured into rivers, these chemicals can hurt wild animals, birds, fish, and people. Steam from a geothermal well often smells awful, like rotten eggs, because of the sulfur. The best way to avoid pollution from hot springs' mineral water is to put the water back where it came from, pumping it back into the aquifer once its heat has been used up. But since hot springs are usually found where there are many earthquakes and a lot of volcanic activity, the pipes that are used must be strong and flexible to prevent breakage.

HOT DRY ROCKS

Many parts of the world have hot rocks close enough to the surface to use, but no underground water supplies to bring the heat to the surface. After a sudden rise in oil prices in 1973, scientists began looking for ways to use this heat.

Hot dry rock (HDR) energy schemes are still only at the experimental stage, but they are a promising idea for the future.

The rocks that get hottest, such as granite, are hard crystals.

Below: Geothermal energy is concentrated within the Ring of Fire. Here, natural hot water can be used in people's homes.

Opposite page: Where natural hot water cannot be used, hot dry rock schemes can provide people with hot water and electricity.

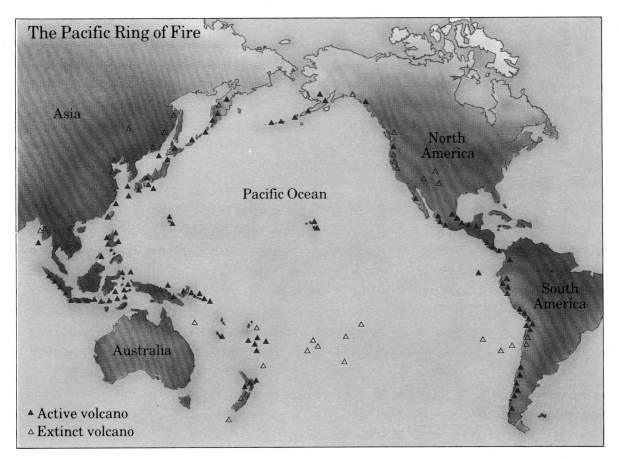

The Pacific Ring of Fire

Asia

North America

Pacific Ocean

South America

Australia

▲ Active volcano
△ Extinct volcano

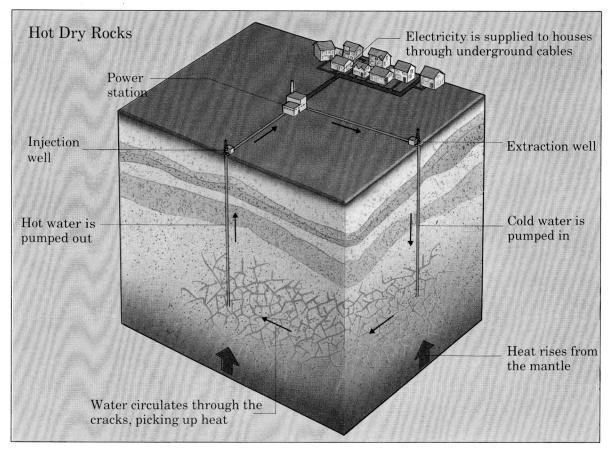

Hot Dry Rocks

Electricity is supplied to houses through underground cables

Power station

Injection well

Extraction well

Hot water is pumped out

Cold water is pumped in

Heat rises from the mantle

Water circulates through the cracks, picking up heat

These can be as hot as 554°F (290°C). This is a vast store of energy, but it is not easy to use. In HDR schemes, two deep holes are drilled in the rock several hundred yards apart. To widen the cracks between them, liquid is pumped down the holes at very high pressure. Large amounts of water are then pumped down one hole, called the **injection well**, to fill up the spaces and create an artificial reservoir.

The water is heated by the hot rocks, then pumped back to the surface through the other hole, called the **extraction well**. Here it turns into steam, which drives a turbine and produces electricity. When it has turned back into water, it is pumped down the injection well to be reheated, and the cycle begins once again.

The problem with HDR schemes is that the holes for the injection well and the extraction well both have to be very deep. It takes expensive machinery to drill holes that deep. To keep the wells from collapsing, the holes have to be lined with pipes. All this takes a lot of time and money. It's actually cheaper to drill for oil instead. But one day, when all our oil is gone, hot dry rocks may make up some of the energy loss.

There are still many problems to overcome, but in Great Britain, for example, HDR schemes could provide as much as 10 percent of the country's electricity in the future.

An experimental power plant was begun in 1976 at Rosemanowes, near the southwestern tip of England, that may one day provide energy for towns in that region.

A drilling rig bores deep below a granite quarry at Rosemanowes, England, to reach the hot rocks below.

This experimental HDR power station pumps cold water into deep hot rocks and then brings hot water back to the surface.

One of the main test sites for HDR energy is at Fenton Hill, New Mexico. Although the water taken from the extraction well here was not hot enough to turn into steam, engineers found a way to solve this problem. They used the hot water to heat a liquid called Freon.

It takes much less heat to turn Freon into steam than it does water. So hot water from the ground was used to heat the Freon, which turned to steam and turned the turbine. As the hot water cooled, it was pumped back underground to pick up more heat. When the Freon gas cooled, it turned back into liquid and could be used over and over again. Systems like this one may one day make HDR projects practical, time-efficient, and affordable.

POWER AT WAIRAKEI

New Zealand, on the Ring of Fire, has several volcanoes and many areas of geothermal activity, such as geysers and hot springs. After World War II, the country was suffering from a shortage of electricity. The government decided to try using geothermal energy to produce electricity, following the success of the experimental geothermal power plant at Larderello, Italy.

The search for suitable aquifers began in 1950. Holes of different depths were drilled at several sites in volcanic areas. The engineers who did this work were looking for underground reservoirs which could provide large quantities of hot water.

Wairakei was chosen as the first site in 1950. Engineers and **geologists** moved into the area.

The Wairakei geothermal power station was the first large-scale one of its kind in the world, and it still supplies power today.

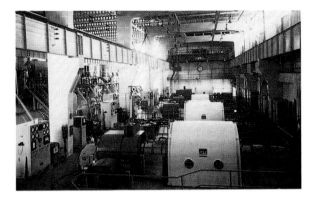

The generator room.

The geologists measured the sizes and temperatures of all the hot springs and geysers at Wairakei and made maps of them. Then they took samples of the water to see what minerals it contained. Airplanes took photographs from the sky which showed the natural cracks in the Earth's surface. The engineers began to drill small test holes to measure the temperatures at different depths.

The tests started small, but by 1954, the engineers had discovered enough steam and hot water to produce electricity for 13,500 people. One well was like an artificial geyser, and had enough pressure to shoot water over 300 feet (91 m) into the air. The government decided to go ahead with the building of a large power plant, and the first turbines were ordered. In 1955, large drilling rigs were used to start drilling sixty wells for the power plant.

A turbine attached to a generator was placed at the top of each well. The Wairakei geothermal power plant began producing electricity for New Zealanders in 1958.

Not every nation is lucky enough to have a large area full of geothermal energy. But for those that do, the Wairakei power plant shows how geothermal energy can help meet their energy needs. In a future world that makes better use of its natural resources, geothermal energy can play an important part by providing heat and electricity for millions of people.

Drilling continues today.

You will need:

- Two bricks
- A metal can with a resealable lid (like a cocoa tin or tea canister)
- A piece of wire from a coat hanger
- String
- Two Popsicle sticks
- A little modeling clay
- A short, thick candle
- Thick aluminum foil
- Scissors, a pencil, a saucer, and a glass

How to make your own turbine:

1. Get an adult to make a small hole in the middle of the lid.

2. Notch the Popsicle sticks and tie them tightly to opposite sides of the can with the string.

3. Pour half an inch (about 1 cm) of water into the can and put the lid on snugly.

4. Carefully cut the foil into a circle, using the saucer as an outline. Draw a smaller circle inside it, using the glass. Draw

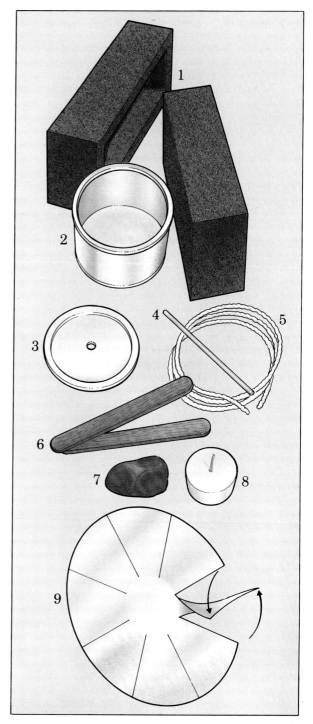

28

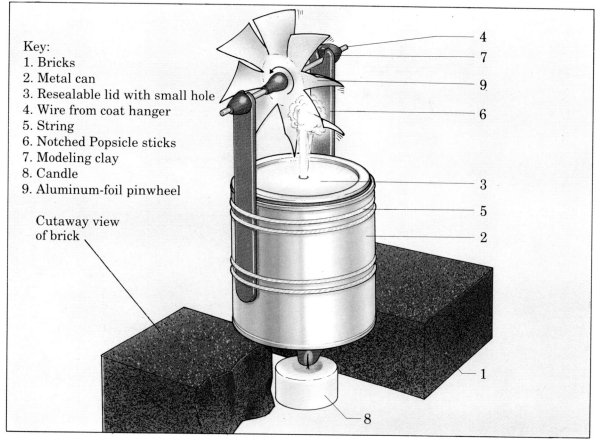

Key:
1. Bricks
2. Metal can
3. Resealable lid with small hole
4. Wire from coat hanger
5. String
6. Notched Popsicle sticks
7. Modeling clay
8. Candle
9. Aluminum-foil pinwheel

Cutaway view of brick

lines from the edge to the inner circle, dividing the space between into eight equal parts, like the petals of a flower.

5. Cut along the lines to separate the "petals." Be sure that they stay firmly attached to the uncut center circle.

6. Give the "petals" a little twist to make the pinwheel shape shown in the diagram.

7. Push the wire through the center of the foil pinwheel. Use some modeling clay to fasten the wire to the Popsicle sticks. Put some clay on either side of the pinwheel to keep it over the lid's hole, but be sure that the pinwheel can spin freely.

8. Put the candle between the two bricks and ask an adult to light it for you. Carefully place the can on top. After a few minutes, steam should start to come out of the hole in the lid and turn the pinwheel.

Warning:

Steam is hot! Don't touch the jet of steam, the candle flame, or the hot can, or you may get burned. Remember that the can is still hot after the flame has gone out.

Glossary

Acid rain: Rain formed when pollution in the air combines with water vapor in clouds. It kills trees and wildlife, and, in time, will even eat away stone.

Aquifer: A natural underground layer of rock that holds and stores water.

Atmosphere: The layer of gases that surrounds a planet, moon, or star.

Diversify: To give variety to something; to rely on energy from a wide variety of sources, rather than to depend on just a few sources.

Extraction well: In hot dry rock energy schemes, a very deep hole in the ground from which steam is taken.

Fossil fuels: Fuels, such as coal and natural gas, that formed from plants and animals that lived millions of years ago.

Generator: A machine that generates, or produces, electricity.

Geologist: A person who studies the Earth and its rocks.

Geothermal energy: Energy from the natural heat that escapes from inside the Earth.

Geyser: A jet of hot water and steam that shoots into the air.

Greenhouse effect: The warming of the Earth due to gases in the atmosphere that trap the Sun's heat.

Injection well: In hot dry rock energy schemes, a very deep hole in the ground into which cold water is pumped.

Minerals: Dissolved substances found in water from hot springs; also, any materials from the Earth that are not animal or vegetable, such as granite, coal, or sulfur.

Molten: Melted. Magma is molten rock.

Nuclear energy: Energy produced by splitting or combining atoms.

Porous: Allowing water and other liquids to pass through easily.

Reservoir: A place where water is "reserved," or stored.

Ring of Fire: The shores of the Pacific Ocean, so called because of all the volcanoes and hot springs that are found there.

Spa: A health resort where people go to soak in and to drink warm mineral water.

Turbine: A device, shaped somewhat like a propeller, which turns to power an electric generator.

Books to Read

Earth Power: The Story of Geothermal Energy. Madeleine
    Yates (Abingdon)
Energy. Andrew Langley (Franklin Watts)
Energy: Making It Work. Tom Johnston (Gareth Stevens)
Energy from the Earth. (National Geographic)
Fuel and Energy. Herta S. Breiter (Raintree)
Geothermal Energy: A Hot Prospect. Augusta Goldin
    (Harcourt Brace Jovanovich)
Heat and Energy. Kathryn Whyman (Franklin Watts)
Tapping the Earth's Heat. Patricia Lauber (Garrard)
Young Scientists Explore: An Encyclopedia of Energy Activities.
    Jerry DeBruin (Good Apple)

Places to Write

These groups can help you find out more about geothermal energy and
alternative energy in general. When you write, be sure to ask specific
questions, and always include your full name, address, and age.

In the United States:

**Conservation and Renewable
    Energy Inquiry and
    Referral Service**
P.O. Box 8900
Silver Spring, MD   20907

**Alternative Energy Resources
    Organization**
44 Last Chance Gulch
Helena, MT   59601

In Canada:

**Efficiency and Alternative
    Energy Technology Board
Department of Energy,
    Mines, and Resources**
580 Booth Street, 7th Floor
Ottawa, Ontario   K1A 0E4

**Canadian Earth Energy
    Association**
2978 Barlow Crescent
Dunrobin, Ontario   K0A 1T0

Index

A **boldface** number means
that the entry is illustrated
on that page.